D1563729

The Devil's Dictionary

SELECTIONS FROM

The Devil's Dictionary

BY
Ambrose Bierce

DECORATED BY
John Miles

Þ

PARSIMONY PRESS
2000

Selections from the Devil's Dictionary
Parsimony Press Limited
ISBN 1-902979-06-0

Illustrations & biography copyright
© Parsimony Press Limited 2000

First published in Great Britain in 2000
Second impression 2000
Parsimony Press Ltd
West Huntspill, Somerset

Typeset by Wragge Industries
Designed by John Miles
Colour Reproduction by Vimnice International, Hong Kong
Printed and bound by LEGO SpA, Italy

There is a great deal more to Ambrose
Gwinett Bierce than meets the eye.

We learn that he was born on June 24th in
1842 in Horse Creek Cave in Meig's County
in Ohio. He was the tenth of thirteen children
born to two proud parents, a Puritan mother
and a Calvinist father, each of whom could
trace their families back to the earliest
settlers. Only ten of the children survived
infancy. It was a meagre existence for all of
them, possibly because his father was too
interested in the study of classics to devote as
much time to the farm as was needed, and
probably because neither parent was
temperamentally suited to so rural an
existence.

He was only nineteen when he was caught up
in the American Civil War (1861-65).
Although at first he was glad to have left
home his first exposure to battle was Shiloh.
During the following years he was in many
more battles, was twice wounded and was
also once captured by the Confederates. This
terrible long-drawn conflict resulted in the
death of more soldiers than all the wars that
the United States has been in since then, and

scarred the minds of too many of the survivors.

Some of the time during these years Bierce scouted alone behind enemy lines mapping positions that could be useful to the Union armies. One of his most moving stories *An Occurrence at Owl Creek Bridge* casts the Union scout as the villain of the piece. By the end of the war he had reached the rank of major, but was so thoroughly embittered by the experience that it appears to have affected the rest of his life and the way he looked at it. He said his role in the war was like being a paid assassin. He became known as 'Bitter Bierce'.

After the war he was given perhaps a more dangerous job as a Treasury agent in an effort to prevent the shipping of contraband cotton in the South, where Union soldiers were not among the most popular, and interfering Union soldiers fair game for almost anybody.

He was rescued from this by being offered a job by his old commanding officer in an expedition mapping western territory. When in California he was offered a permanent commission. As it was only as a lieutenant he resigned and started his long career in journalism.

He was almost an instant success writing for papers, helping to start up literary magazines, and living and working with like-minded people. It was during this period in California that he met and began mixing with such people as Bret Harte and Mark Twain.

Ambrose Bierce is still known chiefly as a short story writer and one of his best-known books, *The Fiend's Delight* was published at the end of this period, when, aged thirty, he went to England. He lived in England for four years – though some say only two – and it was here that another of his books, *Cobwebs from an Empty Skull* appeared in 1874. He also wrote humorous pieces which earned him a reputation in London as great as that of Mark Twain.

 In 1876 he returned to California and re-entered a career as a journalist, working for William Randolph Hearst. For more than twenty years this was his life. In 1897 he moved to Washington as Hearst's Washington correspondent, and it seems that as he grew older he became even less enchanted by both the human race and himself as part of it. Nevertheless it was during his years in Washington that he completed a selection of his writing that was later published in twelve volumes as his *Collected Works.*

As he grew older opinions on his place in American literature were divided. On the one hand he was called 'the only American who was a complete man of letters' while on the other, there was a critic who valued his *Collected Works* only for the excellence of the binding.

In 1913, when he was 71, and estranged from the remnants of his family, he went to Mexico, where another civil war was raging. He was not heard of again, and is generally assumed to have died or been killed in 1914. His last letter was postmarked December 26th 1913. Some think he may have died of the asthma that plagued him for much of his life. Some even suggest that he returned to Europe and became involved in the Great War.

To us is the thought that of the four million

words he wrote during his life only about a quarter remains, and most of that is pretty hard to find.

It was in 1906 that he published *The Cynic's Word Book*, which was later expanded to be *The Devil's Dictionary*, which took one of the twelve books of his Collected Works. Nearly a hundred years later there are few of the sardonic definitions that we have chosen that don't ring as true today as they did then.

abscond, *v.i.* to 'move in a mysterious way,' commonly with the property of another.

Spring beckons! All things to the call respond
The trees are leaving and cashiers abscond.
PHELA ORM

abstainer, *n.* A weak person who yields to the temptation of denying himself a pleasure. A total abstainer is one who abstains from everything but abstention, and especially from inactivity in the affairs of others.

Said a man to a crapulent youth: 'I thought
You a total abstainer, my son.'
'So I am, so I am,' said the scapegrace caught –
'But not, sir, a bigoted one.'
G.J.

absurdity, *n.* A statement or belief manifestly inconsistent with one's own opinion.

accuse, *v.t.* To affirm another's guilt or unworth; most commonly as a justification of ourselves for having wronged him.

acquaintance, *n.* A person whom we know well enough to borrow from, but not well enough to lend to. A degree of friendship called slight when its object is poor or obscure, and intimate when he is rich or famous.

admiration, *n.* Our polite recognition of another's resemblance to ourselves.

alliance, *n.* In international politics, the union of two thieves who have their hands so deeply inserted in each other's pockets that they cannot separately plunder the third.

amnesty, *n.* The state's magnanimity to those offenders whom it would be too expensive to punish.

anoint, *v.t.* To grease a king or other great functionary already sufficiently slippery.

As sovereigns are anointed by the priesthood
So pigs to lead the populace are greased good.
JUDIBRAS

apologize, *v.i.* To lay the foundation for future offence.

appeal, *v.t.* In law, to put the dice into the box for another throw.

architect, *n.* One who drafts a plan of your house, and plans a draft of your money.

arrest, *v.t.* Formally to detain one accused of unusualness.

God made the world in six days and was arrested on the seventh.   *The Unauthorized Version*

auctioneer, *n.* The man who proclaims with a hammer that he has picked a pocket with his tongue.

Bacchus, *n.* A convenient deity invented by the ancients as an excuse for getting drunk.

Is public worship, then, a sin,
That for devotions paid to Bacchus
The lictors dare to run us in,
And resolutely thump and wack us?

bait, *n.* A preparation that renders the hook more palatable. The best kind is beauty.

barometer, *n.* An ingenious instrument which indicates what kind of weather we are having.

barrack, *n.* A house in which soldiers enjoy a portion of that of which it is their business to deprive others.

belladonna, *n.* In Italian a beautiful lady; in English a deadly poison. A striking example of the essential identity of the two tongues.

bigot, *n.* One who is obstinately and zealously attached to an opinion that you do not entertain.

bore, *n.* A person who talks when you wish him to listen.

boundary, *n.* In political geography, an imaginary line between two nations, separating the imaginary rights of one from the imaginary rights of the other.

bride, *n.* A woman with a fine prospect of happiness behind her.

cabbage, *n.* A familiar kitchen-garden vegetable about as large and wise as a man's head.

The cabbage is so called from Cabagius, a prince who on ascending the throne issued a decree appointing a High Council of Empire consisting of the members of his predecessor's Ministry and the cabbages in the royal garden. When any of his Majesty's measures of state policy miscarried conspicuously it was gravely announced that several members of the High Council had been beheaded, and his murmuring subjects were appeased.

circus, *n.* A place where horses, ponies and elephants are permitted to see men, women and children acting the fool.

clairvoyant, *n.*

A person, commonly a woman, who has the power of seeing that which is invisible to her patron – namely, that he is a blockhead.

clergyman, *n.* A man who undertakes the management of our spiritual affairs as a method of bettering his temporal ones.

confidant, confidante, *n.* One entrusted by A with secrets of B, confided by *him* to C.

congratulation, *n.* the civility of envy.

connoisseur, *n.* A specialist who knows everything about something, and nothing about anything else.

An old wine-bibber having been smashed in a railway collision, some wine was poured upon his lips to revive him. 'Pauillac, 1873,' he murmured and died.

conservative, *n.* A statesman who is enamored of existing evils, as distinguished from the Liberal, who wishes to replace them with others.

consolation, *n.* The knowledge that a better man is more unfortunate than yourself.

consult, *v.t.* To seek another's approval of a course already decided on.

conversation, *n.* A fair for the display of the minor mental commodities, each exhibitor being too intent upon the arrangement of his own wares to observe those of his neighbor.

corporation, *n.* An ingenious device for obtaining individual profit without individual responsibility.

coward, *n.* One who in a perilous emergency thinks with his legs.

craft, *n.* A fool's substitute for brains.

dawn, *n.* The time when men of reason go to bed. Certain old men prefer to rise at about that time, taking a cold bath and a long walk with an empty stomach, and otherwise mortifying the flesh. They then point with pride to these practices as the cause of their sturdy health and ripe years; the truth being that they are hearty and old, not because of their habits, but in spite of them. The reason we find only robust persons doing this thing is that it has killed all the others who have tried it.

decalogue, *n.* A series of commandments, ten in number – just enough to permit an intelligent selection for observance, but not enough to embarrass the choice. Following is the revised edition of the Decalogue, calculated for this meridian.

Thou shalt no God but me adore:
'Twere too expensive to have more.

No images nor idols make
For Robert Ingersoll to break.

Take not God's name in vain; select
A time when it will have effect.

Work not on Sabbath days at all,
But go to see the teams play ball.

Honor thy parents. That creates
For life insurance better rates.

Kill not, abet not those who kill;
Thou shalt not pay thy butcher's bill.

Kiss not thy neighbor's wife, unless
Thine own thy neighbor doth caress.

Don't steal; thou'lt never thus compete
Successfully in business. Cheat.

Bear not false witness – that is low –
But 'hear 'tis rumored so and so.'

Covet thou naught that thou hast not
By hook or crook, or somehow, got.   G.J.

decide, *v.i.* To succumb to the preponderance of one set of influences over another set.

A leaf was riven from a tree.
'I mean to fall to earth,' said he.

The west wind, rising, made him veer.
'Eastward,' said he, 'I now shall steer.'

The east wind rose with greater force.
Said he: ''Twere wise to change my course.'

With equal power they contend.
He said: 'My judgment I suspend.'

Down died the winds; the leaf, elate,
Cried: 'I've decided to fall straight.'

'First thoughts are best?' That's not the moral;
Just choose your own and we'll not quarrel.

Howe'er your choice may chance to fall,
You'll have no hand in it at all.   G.J.

dentist, *n.* A prestidigitator who, putting metal into your mouth, pulls coins out of your pocket.

destiny, *n.* A tyrant's authority for crime and a fool's excuse for failure.

diagnosis, *n.* A physician's forecast of disease by the patient's pulse and purse.

diaphragm, *n.* A muscular partition separating disorders from the chest from disorders from the bowels.

diary, *n.* A daily record of that part of one's life which he can relate to himself without blushing.

Hearst kept a diary wherein were writ
All that he had of wisdom and of wit.
So the Recording Angel, when Hearst died,
Erased all entries of his own and cried:
'I'll judge you by your diary.' Said Hearst:

'Thank you; 'twill show you I am Saint the
First'–
Straightway producing, jubilant and proud,
That record from a pocket in his shroud.
The Angel slowly turned the pages o'er,
Each stupid line of which he knew before,
Glooming and gleaming as by turns he hit
On shallow sentiment and stolen wit;
Then gravely closed the book and gave it back.
'My friend, you've wandered from your proper
track;
You'd never be content this side of the tomb –
For big ideas Heaven has little room,
And Hell's no latitude for making mirth,'
He said, and kicked the fellow back to earth.

'THE MAD PHILOSOPHER.'

dictionary, *n.* A malevolent literary device
for cramping the growth of a language and
making it hard and inelastic. This
dictionary, however, is a most useful work.

diplomacy, *n.* The patriotic art of lying for
one's country.

distance, *n.* The only thing that the rich are
willing for the poor to call theirs, and keep.

distress, *n.* A disease incurred by exposure
to the prosperity of a friend.

economy, *n.* Purchasing the barrel of whiskey that you do not need for the price of the cow that you cannot afford.

education, *n.* That which discloses to the wise and disguises from the foolish their lack of understanding.

egotist, *n.* A person of low taste, more interested in himself than in me.

> *Megaceph, chosen to serve the State*
> *In the halls of legislative debate,*
> *One day with all his credentials came*
> *To the capitol's door and announced his name.*
> *The doorkeeper looked, with a comical twist*
> *Of the face, at the eminent egotist,*
> *And said: 'Go away, for we settle here*
> *All manner of questions, knotty and queer,*
> *And we cannot have, when the speaker demands*
> *To be told how every member stands,*
> *A man who to all things under the sky*
> *Assents by eternally voting "I".'*

elegy, *n.* A composition in verse, in which, without employing any of the methods of humor, the writer aims to produce in the reader's mind the dampest kind of dejection. The most famous English example begins somewhat like this:

The cur foretells the knell of parting day;
The loafing herd winds slowly o'er the lea;
The wise man homeward plods; I only stay
to fiddle-faddle in a minor key.

eloquence, *n.*
The art of orally persuading fools that white is the color that it appears to be. It includes the gift of making any color appear white.

emotion, *n.* A prostrating disease caused by a determination of the heart to the head. It is sometimes accompanied by a copious discharge of hydrated chloride of sodium from the eyes.

epaulet, *n.* An ornamented badge, serving to distinguish a military officer from the enemy – that is to say, from the officer of lower rank to whom his death would give promotion.

exile, *n.* One who serves his country by residing abroad, yet is not an ambassador.

An English sea-captain, being asked if he had read *The Exile of Erin*, replied: 'No, sir, but I should like to anchor on it.' Years afterwards, when he had been hanged as a pirate after a career of unparalleled atrocities, the following memorandum was found in the ship's log that he had kept at the time of his reply;

Aug. 3d, 1842. Made a joke on the ex-Isle of Erin. Coldly received. War with the whole world!

experience, *n.* The wisdom that enables us to recognize as an undesirable old acquaintance the folly that we have already embraced.

To one who, journeying through night and fog,
Is mired neck-deep in an unwholesome bog,
Experience, like the rising of the dawn,
Reveals the path that he should not have gone.
JOELFRAD BLINK

faith, *n.* Belief without evidence in what is told by one who speaks without knowledge, of things without parallel.

fiddle, *n.* An instrument to tickle human ears by friction of a horse's tail on the entrails of a cat.

To Rome said Nero: 'If to smoke you turn
I shall not cease to fiddle while you burn.'
To Nero Rome replied: 'Pray do your worst,
'Tis my excuse that you were fiddling first.'

ORM PLUDGE

fidelity, *n.* A virtue peculiar to those who are about to be betrayed.

force, *n.*

'Force is but might,' the teacher said –
'That definition's just.'
The boy said naught but thought instead,
Remembering his pounded head:
'Force is not might but must!'

fork, *n.* An instrument used chiefly for the purpose of putting dead animals into the mouth. Formerly the knife was employed for this purpose, and by many worthy persons is still thought to have many advantages over the other tool, which, however, they do not altogether reject, but use to assist in charging the knife. The immunity of these persons from swift and awful death is one of the most striking proofs of God's mercy to those that hate Him.

friendship, *n.* A ship big enough to carry two in fair weather, but only one in foul.

The sea was calm and the sky was blue;
Merrily, merrily sailed we two.
  (High barometer maketh glad.)
On the tipsy ship, with a dreadful shout,
The tempest descended and we fell out.
 (O the walking is nasty bad!)
                              ARMIT HUFF BETTLE

genealogy, *n.* An account of one's descent from an ancestor who did not particularly care to trace his own.

generous, *adj.* Originally this word meant noble by birth and was rightly applied to a great multitude of persons. It now means noble by nature and is taking a bit of a rest.

gout, *n.* A physician's name for the rheumatism of a rich patient.

grave, *n.* A place in which the dead are laid to await the coming of the medical student.

Beside a lonely grave I stood –
  With brambles 'twas encumbered;
The winds were moaning in the wood,
  Unheard by him who slumbered.

A rustic standing near, I said:
  'He cannot hear it blowing!'
''Course not,' said he: 'the feller's dead –
  He can't hear nowt that's going.'

'Too true,' I said; 'alas, too true –
  No sound his sense can quicken!'
'Well, mister, wot is that to you? –
  The deadster ain't a-kickin'.'

I knelt and prayed: 'O Father, smile
  On him, and mercy show him!'
That countryman looked on him the while,
  And said: 'Ye didn't know him.'

POBETER DUNK

guillotine, *n.* A machine which makes a Frenchman shrug his shoulders with good reason.

In his great work on Divergent Lines of Racial Evolution, the learned Professor Brayfugle argues from the prevalence of this gesture – the shrug – among Frenchmen, that they are descended from turtles and it is simply a survival of the habit of retracting the head inside the shell. It is with reluctance that I differ with so eminent an authority, but in my judgment (as more elaborately set forth and enforced in my work entitled *Hereditary Emotions* - lib. II, c. XI) the shrug is a poor foundation upon which to build so important a theory, for previously to the Revolution the gesture was unknown. I have not a doubt that it is directly referable to the terror inspired by the guillotine during the period of that instrument's activity.

habit, *n.* A shackle for the free.

hag, *n.* An elderly lady whom you do not happen to like; sometimes called, also, a hen, or cat. Old witches, sorceresses, etc., were called hags from the belief that their heads were surrounded by a kind of baleful lumination or nimbus – hag being the popular name of the peculiar electrical light sometimes observed in the hair. At one time hag was not a word of reproach: Drayton speaks of a 'beautiful hag, all smiles,' much as Shakespeare said, 'sweet wench.' It would not now be proper to call your sweetheart a hag – that compliment is reserved for the use of her grandchildren.

hand, *n.*

A singular instrument worn at the end of the human arm and commonly thrust into somebody's pocket.

happiness, *n.* An agreeable sensation arising from contemplating the misery of another.

hatred, *n.* A sentiment appropriate to the occasion of another's superiority.

hers, *pron.* His.

history, *n.* An account mostly false, of events mostly unimportant, which are brought about by rulers mostly knaves, and soldiers mostly fools.

Of Roman history, great Niebuhr's shown
'Tis nine-tenths lying. Faith, I wish 'twere known,
Ere we accept great Niebuhr as a guide,
Wherein he blundered and how much he lied.
SALDER BUPP

homeopathy, *n.* A school of medicine midway between Allopathy and Christian Science. To the last both the others are distinctly inferior, for Christian Science will cure imaginary diseases, and they cannot.

homicide, *n.* The slaying of one human being by another. There are four kinds of homicide: felonious, excusable, justifiable and praiseworthy, but it makes no great difference to the person slain whether he fell by one kind or another – the classification is for advantage of the lawyers.

hospitality, *n.* The virtue which induces us to feed and lodge certain persons who are not in need of food and lodging.

husband, *n.* One who, having dined, is charged with the care of the plate.

hypocrite, *n.* One who, professing virtues that he does not respect, secures the advantage of seeming to be what he despises.

I is the first letter of the alphabet, the first word of the language, the first thought of the mind, the first object of affection. In grammar it is a pronoun of the first person and singular number. Its plural is said to be We, but how there can be more than one myself is doubtless clearer to the grammarians than it is to the author of this incomparable dictionary. Conception of two myselves is difficult, but fine. The frank yet graceful use of 'I' distinguishes a good writer from a bad; the latter carries it with the manner of a thief trying to cloak his loot.

ignoramus, *n.* A person unacquainted with certain kinds of knowledge familiar to yourself, and having certain other kinds that you know nothing about.

Dumble was an ignoramus,
Mumble was for learning famous.
Mumble said one day to Dumble:
'Ignorance should be more humble.
Not a spark have you of knowledge
That was got in any college.'
Dumble said to Mumble: 'Truly
You're self-satisfied unduly.
Of things in college I'm denied
A knowledge – you of all beside.'

BORELLI

imagination, *n.* A warehouse of facts, with poet and liar in joint ownership.

immigrant, *n.* An unenlightened person who thinks one country better than another.

J is a consonant in English, but some nations use it as a vowel – than which nothing could be more absurd. Its original form, which has been but slightly modified, was that of the tail of a subdued dog, and it was not a letter but a character, standing for a Latin verb, jacere, 'to throw' because when a stone is thrown at a dog the dog's tail assumes that shape. This is the origin of the letter, as expounded by the renowned Dr Jocolpus Bumer, of the University of Belgrade, who established his conclusions on the subject in a work of three quarto volumes and committed suicide on being reminded that the j in the Roman alphabet had originally no curl.

jealous, *adj.* Unduly concerned about the preservation of that which can be lost only if not worth keeping.

justice, *n.* A commodity which in a more or less adulterated condition the State sells to the citizen as a reward for his allegiance, taxes and personal service.

kill, *v.t.* To create a vacancy without nominating a successor.

kilt, *n.*
A costume sometimes worn by Scotchmen in America and Americans in Scotland.

kindness, *n.*
A brief preface to ten volumes of exaction.

labor, *n.* One of the processes by which A acquires property for B.

land, *n.* A part of the earth's surface, considered as property. The theory that land is property subject to private ownership and control is the foundation of modern society, and is eminently worthy of the superstructure. Carried to its logical conclusion, it means that some have the right to prevent others from living; for the right to own implies the right exclusively to occupy; and in fact laws of trespass are enacted wherever property in land is recognized. It follows that if the whole area of terra firma is owned by A, B and C, there will be no place for D, E, F and G to be born, or, born as trespassers, to exist.

A life on the ocean wave,
  A home on the rolling deep,
For the spark that nature gave
  I have there the right to keep.
They give me the cat-o'-nine
  Whenever I go ashore.
Then ho! for the flashing brine –
  I'm a natural commodore!   DODLE

lap, *n.* One of the most important organs of the female system – an admirable provision of nature for the repose of infancy, but chiefly useful in rural festivities to support plates of cold chicken and heads of adult males. The male of our species has a rudimentary lap, imperfectly developed and in no way contributing to the animal's substantial welfare.

lawyer, *n*. One skilled in circumvention of the law.

lecturer, *n*. One with his hand in your pocket, his tongue in your ear and his faith in your patience.

litigation, *n*. A machine which you go into as a pig and come out of as a sausage.

marriage, *n.* The state or condition of a community consisting of a master, a mistress and two slaves, making in all, two.

material, *adj.* Having an actual existence, as distinguished from an imaginary one. Important.

Material things I know, or feel, or see;
All else is immaterial to me.

JAMARACH HOLOBOM

mayonnaise, *n.* One of the sauces which serve the French in place of a state religion.

me, *pron.* The objectionable case of I. The personal pronoun in English has three cases, the dominative, the objectionable and the oppressive. Each is all three.

millennium, *n.* The period of a thousand years when the lid is to be screwed down, with all reformers on the under side.

misdemeanor, *n.* An infraction of the law having less dignity than a felony and constituting no claim to admittance into the best criminal society.

By misdemeanors he essayed to climb
Into the aristocracy of crime.
O, woe was him! – with manner chill and grand
'Captains of industry' refused his hand,
'Kings of finance' denied him recognition
And 'railway magnates' jeered his low condition.
He robbed a bank to make himself respected.
They still rebuffed him, for he was detected.

S.V.HANIPUR

miss, *n.* A title with which we brand unmarried women to indicate that they are in the market. Miss, Missis (Mrs) and Mister (Mr) are the three most distinctly disagreeable words in the language, in sound and sense. Two are corruptions of

Mistress, the other of Master. In the general abolition of social titles in this country they miraculously escaped to plague us. If we must have them let us be consistent and give one to the unmarried man. I venture to suggest Mush, abbreviated to Mh.

money, *n.* A blessing that is of no advantage to us excepting when we part with it. An evidence of culture and a passport to polite society. Supportable property.

mouth, *n.* In man, the gateway to the soul; in woman, the outlet of the heart.

mythology, *n.* The body of a primitive people's beliefs concerning its origin, early history, heroes, deities and so forth, as distinguished from the true accounts which it invents later.

neighbor, *n.* One whom we are commanded to love as ourselves, and who does all he knows how to make us disobedient.

nepotism, *n.* Appointing your grandmother to office for the good of the party.

noise, *n.* A stench in the ear. Undomesticated music. The chief product and authenticating sign of civilization.

nominee, *n.* A modest gentleman shrinking from the distinction of private life and diligently seeking the honorable obscurity of public office.

nonsense, *n.* The objections that are urged against this excellent dictionary.

oblivion, *n.* The state or condition in which the wicked cease from struggling and the dreary are at rest. Fame's eternal dumping ground. Cold storage for high hopes. A place where ambitious authors meet their works without pride and their betters without envy. A dormitory without an alarm clock.

obsolete, *adj.* No longer used by the timid. Said chiefly of words. A word which some lexicographer has marked obsolete is ever thereafter an object of dread and loathing to the fool writer, but if it is a good word and has no exact modern equivalent equally good, it is good enough for the good writer. Indeed, a writer's attitude toward 'obsolete' words is as true a measure of his literary ability as anything except the character of his work. A dictionary of obsolete and obsolescent words would not only be singularly rich in strong and sweet parts of speech; it would add large possessions to the vocabulary of every competent writer who might not happen to be a competent reader.

ocean, *n.* A body of water occupying about two-thirds of a world made for man – who has no gills.

once, *adv.* Enough.

opportunity, *n.* A favorable occasion for grasping a disappointment.

ostrich, *n.* A large bird to which (for its sins, doubtless) nature has denied that hinder toe in which so many pious naturalists have seen a conspicuous evidence of design. The absence of a good working pair of wings is no defect, for, as has been ingeniously pointed out, the ostrich does not fly.

pain, *n.* An uncomfortable frame of mind that may have a physical basis in something that is being done to the body, or may be purely mental, caused by the good fortune of another.

palmistry, *n.* The 947th method (according to Mimbleshaw's classification) of obtaining money by false pretences. It consists in 'reading character' in the wrinkles

PALMISTRY

made by closing the hand. The pretence is not altogether false; character can really be read very accurately in this way, for the wrinkles in every hand submitted plainly spell the word 'dupe.' The imposture consists in not reading it aloud.

pantheism, *n.* The doctrine that everything is God, in contradistinction to the doctrine that God is everything.

patience, *n.* A minor form of despair, disguised as a virtue.

patriotism, *n.* Combustible rubbish ready for the torch of any one ambitious to illuminate his name. In Dr Johnson's famous dictionary patriotism is defined as the last resort of a scoundrel. With all due respect to an enlightened but inferior lexicographer I beg to submit that it is the first.

peace, *n.* In international affairs, a period of cheating between two periods of fighting.

philosophy, *n.* A route of many roads leading from nowhere to nothing.

pigmy, *n.* One of a tribe of very small men found by ancient travelers in many parts of the world, but by modern in Central Africa only. The Pigmies are so called to distinguish them from the bulkier Caucasians – who are Hogmies.

plan, *v.t.* To bother about the best method of accomplishing an accidental result.

politician, *n.* An eel in the fundamental mud upon which the superstructure of organized society is reared. When he wriggles he mistakes the agitation of his tail for the trembling of the edifice. As compared with the statesman, he suffers the disadvantage of being alive.

prescription, *n.* A physician's guess at what will best prolong the situation with least harm to the patient.

present, *n.* That part of eternity dividing the domain of disappointment from the realm of hope.

proof, *n.* Evidence having a shade more of plausibility than of unlikelihood. The testimony of two credible witnesses as opposed to that of only one.

queen, *n.*
A woman by
whom the
realm is
ruled when
there is a
king, and
through
whom it is
ruled when
there is not.

quixotic, *adj.*
Absurdly chivalric, like Don Quixote. An
insight into the beauty and excellence of
this incomparable adjective is unhappily
denied to him who has the misfortune to
know that the gentleman's name is
pronounced Ke-ho-tay.

*When ignorance from out our lives can banish
Philology, 'tis folly to know Spanish.*
                                        JUAN SMITH

quotient, *n.* A number showing how many
times a sum of money belonging to one
person is contained in the pocket of another
– usually about as many times as it can be
got there.

radicalism, *n.* The conservatism of tomorrow injected into the affairs of today.

rank, *n.* Relative elevation in the scale of human worth.

> *He held at court a rank so high*
> *That other noblemen asked why.*
> *'Because' 'twas answered, 'others lack*
> *His skill to scratch the royal back.'*
>
> ARAMIS JUKES

rarebit, *n.* A Welsh rabbit, in the speech of the humorless, who point out that it is not a rabbit. To whom it may be solemnly explained that the comestible known as  toad-in-the-hole is not really a toad, and that *riz-de-veau à la financière* is not the smile of a calf prepared after the recipe of a she banker.

rational, *adj.* Devoid of all delusions save those of observation, experience and reflection.

recollect, *v.* To recall with additions something not previously known.

reconsider, *v.* To seek a justification for a decision already made.

referendum, *n.* A law for the submission of proposed legislation to a popular vote to learn the nonsensus of public opinion.

riot, *n.* A popular entertainment given to the military by innocent bystanders.

saw, *n*. A trite popular saying, or proverb. (Figurative and colloquial.) So called because it makes its way into a wooden head. Following are examples of old saws fitted with new teeth.

A penny saved is a penny to squander.

A man is known by the company that he organizes.

A bad workman quarrels with the man who calls him that.

A bird in the hand is worth what it will bring.

Better late than before anybody has invited you.

Example is better than following it.

Half a loaf is better than a whole one if there is much else.

Think twice before you speak to a friend in need.

What is worth doing is worth the trouble of asking somebody to do it.

Least said is soonest disavowed.

He laughs best who laughs least.

Speak of the Devil and he will hear about it.

Of two evils choose to be the least.

Strike while your employer has a big contract.

Where there's a will there's a won't.

scriptures, *n.* The sacred books of our holy religion, as distinguished from the false and profane writings on which all other faiths are based.

self-evident, *adj.* Evident to one's self and to nobody else.

selfish, *adj.* Devoid of consideration for the selfishness of others.

serial, *n.*
A literary work, usually a story that is not true, creeping through several issues of a newspaper or magazine.

Frequently appended to each instalment is a 'synopsis of preceding chapters' for those who have not read them, but a direr need is a synopsis of succeeding chapters for those who do not intend to read them. A synopsis of the entire work would be still better.

The late James F. Bowman was writing a serial tale for a weekly paper in collaboration with a genius whose name has not come down to us. They wrote, not jointly but alternately, Bowman supplying the instalment for one week, his friend for the next, and so on, world without end, they hoped. Unfortunately they quarrelled, and one Monday morning when Bowman read the paper to prepare himself for his task, he found his work cut out for him in a way to surprise and pain him. His collaborator had embarked every character of the narrative on a ship and sunk them all in the deepest part of the Atlantic.

slang, *n.* The grunt of the human hog (*Pignoramus intolerabilis*) with an audible memory. The speech of one who utters with his tongue what he thinks with his ear, and feels the pride of a creator in accomplishing the feat of a parrot. A means (under Providence) of setting up as a wit without a capital of sense.

table d'hôte, *n.* A caterer's thrifty concession to the universal passion for irresponsibility.

Old Paunchinello, freshly wed,
Took Madame P. to table
And there deliriously fed
As fast as he was able.

'I dote upon good grub,' he cried,
Intent upon its throatage.
'Ah, yes,' said the neglected bride,
'You're in your table d'hotage.'

ASSOCIATED POETS

take, *v.t.* To acquire, frequently by force but preferably by stealth.

technicality, *n.* In an English court a man named Home was tried for slander in having accused a neighbor of murder. His exact words were: 'Sir Thomas Holt hath taken a cleaver and stricken his cook upon the head, so that one side of the head fell upon one shoulder and the other side upon the other shoulder.' The defendant was acquitted by instruction of the court, the learned judges holding that the words did not charge murder, for they did not affirm the death of the cook, that being only an inference.

telephone, *n.*
An invention of the devil which abrogates some of the advantages of making a disagreeable person keep his distance.

telescope, *n.*
A device having a relation to the eye similar to that of the telephone to the ear, enabling distant objects to plague us with a multitude of needless details. Luckily it is unprovided with a bell summoning us to the sacrifice.

twice, *adv.* Once too often.

ugliness, *n.* A gift
of the gods to
certain women,
entailing virtue
without humility.

unction, *n.*
An oiling, or
greasing. The
rite of extreme
unction consists in
touching with oil

consecrated by a bishop several parts of the
body of one engaged in dying. Marbury
relates that after the rite had been
administered to a certain wicked English
nobleman it was discovered that the oil had
not been properly consecrated and no other
could be obtained. When informed of this
the sick man said in anger: 'Then I'll be
damned if I die!' 'My son,' said the priest,
'that is what we fear.'

valor, *n.* A soldierly compound of vanity, duty and the gambler's hope.

virtues, *n.pl.* Certain abstentions.

vituperation, *n.* Satire, as understood by dunces and all such as suffer from an impediment in their wit.

vote, *n.* The instrument and symbol of a freeman's power to make a fool of himself and a wreck of his country.

weaknesses, *n.pl.* Certain primal powers of Tyrant Woman wherewith she holds dominion over the male of her species, binding him to the service of her will and paralyzing his rebellious energies.

wedding, *n.* A ceremony at which two persons undertake to become one, one undertakes to become nothing, and nothing undertakes to become supportable.

wheat, *n.* A cereal from which a tolerably good whisky can with some difficulty be made, and which is also used for bread. The French are said to eat more  bread per capita of population that any other people, which is natural, for only they know how to make the stuff palatable.

wit, *n.* The salt with which the American humorist spoils his intellectual cookery by leaving it out.

witch, *n.*

  1. An ugly and repulsive old woman, in a wicked league with the devil.

  2. A beautiful and attractive young woman, in wickedness a league beyond the devil.

wrath, *n.* Anger of a superior quality and degree, appropriate to exalted characters and momentous occasions; as, 'the wrath of God', 'the day of wrath,' etc. Amongst the ancients the wrath of kings was deemed sacred, for it could usually command the agency of some god for its manifestation, as could also that of a priest. The Greeks before Troy were so harried by Apollo that they jumped out of the frying pan of the wrath of Chryses into the fire of the wrath of Achilles, though Agamemnon, the sole offender, was neither fried nor roasted. A similar noted immunity was that of David when he incurred the wrath of Yahveh by numbering his people, seventy thousand of whom paid the penalty with their lives. God is now Love, and a director of the census performs his work without apprehension of disaster.

X in our alphabet being a needless letter has an added invincibility to the attacks of the spelling reformers, and like them, will doubtless last as long as the language. X is the sacred symbol of ten dollars, and in such words as Xmas, Xn, etc., stands for Christ, not, as is popularly supposed, because it represents a cross, but because the corresponding letter in the Greek alphabet is the initial of his name - Χριστός If it represented a cross it would stand for St Andrew, who testified upon one of that shape. In the algebra of psychology x stands for Woman's mind. Words beginning with X are Grecian and will not be defined in this standard English dictionary.

year, *n.* A period of three hundred and sixty-five disappointments.

yesterday, *n.* The infancy of youth, the youth of manhood, the entire past of age.

But yesterday I should have thought me blest
To stand high-pinnacled upon the peak
Of middle life and look adown the bleak
And unfamiliar foreslope to the West,
Where solemn shadows all the land invest
And stilly voices, half-remembered, speak
Unfinished prophecy, and witch-fires freak
The haunted twilight of the Dark of Rest.
Yea, yesterday my soul was all aflame
To stay the shadow on the dial's face
At manhood's noonmark! Now, in God His name
I chide aloud the little interspace
Disparting me from Certitude, and fain
Would know the dream and vision ne'er again.
BARUCH ARNEGRIFF

It is said that in his last illness the poet Arnegriff was attended at different times by seven doctors.

yoke, *n.* An implement, madam, to whose Latin name, *jugum*, we owe one of the most illuminating words in our language – a word that defines the matrimonial situation with precision, point and poignancy. A thousand apologies for withholding it.

zeal, *n.* A certain nervous disorder afflicting the young and inexperienced. A passion that goeth before a sprawl.

When Zeal sought Gratitude for his reward
He went away exclaiming: 'O my Lord!'
'What do you want?' the Lord asked, bending down.
'An ointment for my cracked and bleeding crown.'

JUM COOPLE

zigzag, *v.t.* To move forward uncertainly, from side to side, as one carrying the white man's burden. (From zed, z, and jag, an Icelandic word of unknown meaning.)

He zedjagged so uncomen wyde
Thet non coude pas on eyder syde;
So, to com saufly thruh, I been
Constreynet for to doodge betwene.

MUNWELE